# THE SLIME QUEEN

# Karina Garcia

RACHAEL L. THOMAS

Checkerboard Library

An Imprint of Abdo Publishing
abdobooks.com

**abdobooks.com**

Published by Abdo Publishing, a division of ABDO, PO Box 398166, Minneapolis, Minnesota 55439. 

Printed in the United States of America, North Mankato, Minnesota
102018
012019

Design and Production: Mighty Media, Inc.
Editor: Katherine Hengel Frankowski
Cover Photographs: Sipa USA/AP Images (center); Mighty Media, Inc.
Interior Photographs: Alamy, pp. 11, 18; AP Images, pp. 5, 29 (middle); David Guo/Flickr, pp. 15 (white glue), 29 (bottom); Emily Berl, p. 23; Getty Images, pp. 17, 19, 27; iStockphoto, pp. 8, 13, 14 (foam balls), 16; Nevit/Wikimedia Commons, pp. 10, 28 (top); Peter Corbett/Flickr, p. 21; Shutterstock, pp. 4, 7, 9, 14 (beads, clay, glitter, shaving cream can, shaving cream), 14–15 (slime), 15 (baking soda, clear glue, contact lens solution, detergent, softener), 20, 24, 25, 26, 29 (top); Sipa USA/AP Images, p. 12; Wikimedia Commons, pp. 6, 28 (bottom)

Library of Congress Control Number: 2018948790

**Publisher's Cataloging-in-Publication Data**

Names: Thomas, Rachael L., author.
Title: The slime queen: Karina Garcia / by Rachael L. Thomas.
Other title: Karina Garcia
Description: Minneapolis, Minnesota : Abdo Publishing, 2019 | Series: Toy trailblazers set 3 | Includes online resources and index.
Identifiers: ISBN 9781532117138 (lib. bdg.) | ISBN 9781532159978 (ebook)
Subjects: LCSH: Do-it-yourself products industry--Juvenile literature. | YouTube (Firm)--Juvenile literature. | Internet videos--Juvenile literature. | Internet Personalities--United States--Biography--Juvenile literature.
Classification: DDC 688.72092 [B]--dc23

# CONTENTS

Chapter 1

# SLIME Sensation

Have you ever plunged your hand into a container of gooey slime? Many people across the world have! In 2016 and 2017, making slime became a global **craze**. Today, there are thousands of slime recipes online. This slime craze began with the help of video **blogger** Karina Garcia.

Garcia was born in California on February 8, 1994. She is a part of a large, Mexican-American family. She grew up with her parents, two sisters, and three brothers.

Growing up, Garcia's family didn't have much. They lived in a small mobile home. Garcia grew up dreaming of one day being able to take care of her parents and **siblings**.

After high school, Garcia attended college but dropped out early. Then she began working as a waitress. During this time, Garcia couldn't decide what to do with her life

Karina Garcia is an expert at making slime. But she also likes to buy it online from other makers! "My house is basically made of slime," she joked.

and career. She felt discouraged and unsure about what to try next.

As a child, Garcia had loved arts and crafts. She also enjoyed science. In 2015, she realized she could combine her passions. That's when she first discovered slime! Slime allowed Garcia to use science and crafting to create something fun. In time, she'd become a successful, full-time YouTuber making a living from slime.

Chapter 2

# TWO HEADS ARE *Better than One*

Today, Garcia is **confident** and comfortable on camera. She has become a video star! But back in 2015, she was not sure about being a YouTuber. She was nervous about filming herself and posting the videos online where everyone could see them.

Garcia's **twin** sister, Mayra, encouraged Garcia to make her own videos. Mayra's opinion mattered a lot to Garcia. At that time, Mayra already had a successful YouTube channel!

Mayra's channel featured videos about how to apply different makeup products and styles. She posted her first video in October 2012. By 2015, Mayra had 80,000 YouTube **subscribers**!

### FUN FACT

Mayra and Garcia are identical twins. They look very similar. Some YouTube fans believe the two video stars are actually the same person!

YouTube

**Makeup tutorials have remained popular on YouTube. In 2017, they made up 34 percent of all beauty-related content on the video site.**

Mayra's success inspired Garcia. In February 2015, Garcia created her own YouTube channel and posted her first video. The video was called "Easy DIY Lipsticks!" It featured a lipstick recipe Garcia had created at home. The recipe called for lip **balm**, lip gloss, and eye shadow.

Mayra used **social media** to promote her sister's YouTube video. Many of Mayra's fans soon **subscribed** to Garcia's channel too. It was Garcia's first step toward becoming a YouTube star!

Chapter 3

# A RECIPE for Success

Garcia was nervous about posting her first YouTube video. But her **confidence** grew thanks to positive viewer feedback. Many people liked her videos! So, Garcia made more. At first, her videos were about creating and wearing makeup. But Garcia soon began making craft videos too.

In her early craft videos, Garcia showed viewers how to make phone cases, **bath bombs**, and pencil erasers. Within six months, she had more than 250,000 YouTube followers!

One day, Garcia was looking for craft ideas on the **social media** website Pinterest. She saw a slime recipe. It looked simple, so Garcia decided to try it out.

Many people find squeezing slime satisfying or relaxing. Some people get these benefits just by watching videos of slime being squished!

With that one slime recipe, Garcia was hooked! She mastered the recipe, then started creating her own. In August 2015, she posted her first slime video on YouTube. In the video, she makes a squishy slime that can be used as soap.

At first, some YouTube fans judged Garcia for making slime. They thought it was a strange thing to do. But Garcia enjoyed making slime, so she ignored these comments. She continued making slime. She began experimenting with slime color, scent, **texture**, and more.

## FUN FACT

Making slime can be a lot of fun. But it's also a science! In May 2014, the American Chemical Society posted a fact sheet and video. Each explained the chemical reaction that causes slime to form.

Chapter 4

# JUST IN SLIME

**Today, there are thousands of slime recipes from many users on** YouTube. But when Garcia first started researching slime, there were very few recipes **available**. She was one of the first people to post interesting slime **tutorials** online. As a result, she became a slime authority before anyone else could.

Some slimes are thick and bouncy, and some are fluffy or stretchy. Others are gooey and drippy!

As more people discovered slime, Garcia's videos received more and more views. In time, their popularity would create a business opportunity for Garcia. This is because popular videos help YouTube sell advertisement space.

Video ads often appear before popular YouTube videos. The more views a video gets, the more YouTube charges advertisers to place an ad! Many companies pay YouTube large amounts of money to advertise on videos they think will receive a lot of views. YouTube then pays a portion to the video's creator.

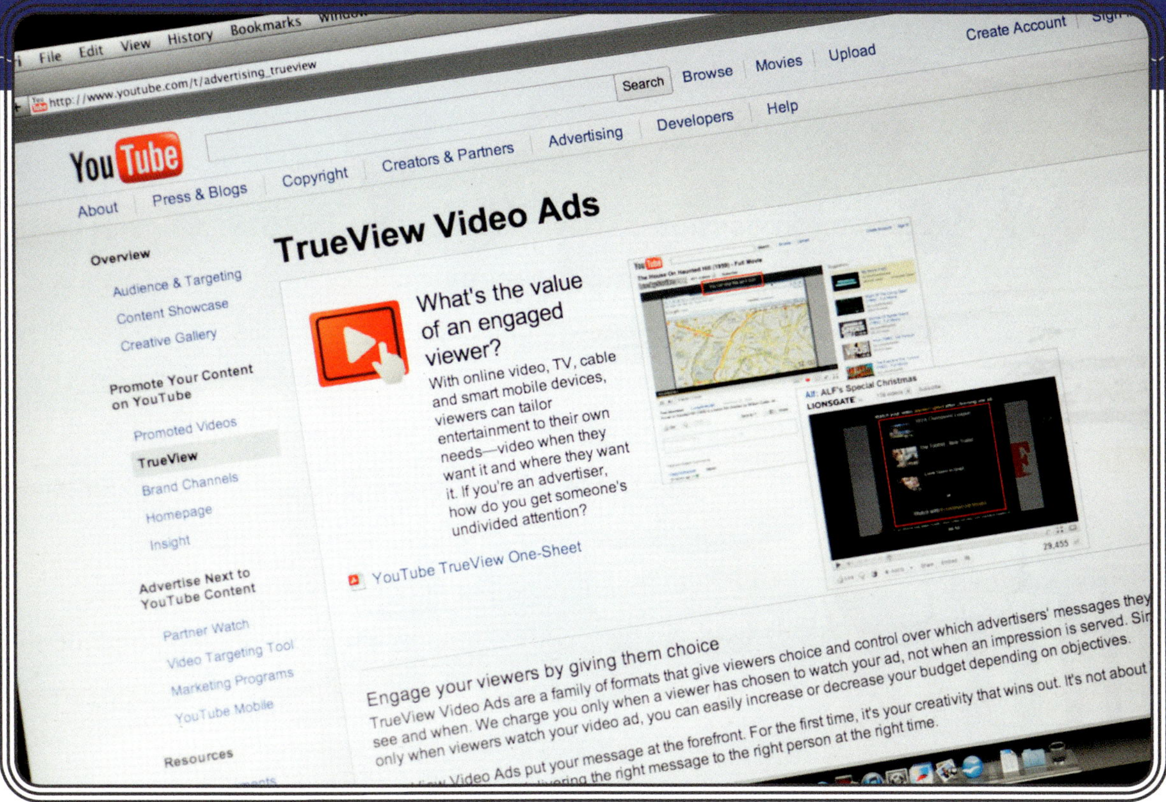


**More than 1 billion people visit YouTube each month. That is a lot of potential customers seeing companies' video ads on popular YouTube videos!**

As Garcia's videos became popular, YouTube started selling video ads on them. That's when YouTube started paying Garcia for her videos. Her first check from YouTube was for about $50. As more and more people watched Garcia's videos, her checks got bigger. Within one year of posting her first video, Garcia received a check for $10,000!

Chapter 5

# SLIME MANIA

**Since Garcia began posting about making slime in 2015, it has become** incredibly popular. For example, **technology** corporation Google keeps track of what people enter into its online search engine. In 2017, "How to make slime" was the most searched how-to phrase of the year in the United States!

Slime fans aren't just watching YouTube videos about making slime. They are actually making their own! Adults and children alike mix up slime by the pound. The slime **craze** has expanded into classrooms too. Many teachers have students make slime as science experiments.

Enthusiasm for slime has even influenced the glue industry. The washable school glue made by craft supply company Elmer's is a main ingredient in many slime recipes. In December 2017, demand for Elmer's glue doubled because so many people

Students in New York make all kinds of slimes during science class.

were using it to make slime. Many parents even complained. There was not enough glue in stores for them to buy for school supplies!

The slime **craze** has not been limited to the United States. It's also popular in France. A glue company near the French town of Tours came very close to **bankruptcy** before slime. Then the slime craze turned the company's fortunes around. The company is now making a huge profit from selling glue!

Chapter 6

# SLIME *Basics*

**Many materials are used to make slime!** But most slime recipes start with glue as the main ingredient. Then, certain slime activators are needed. Finally, slime makers add all kinds of fun ingredients to give slime cool colors, **textures,** and more.

## FUN ADDITIONS

GLITTER

CLAY (MAKES "BUTTER SLIME")

FOAM BALLS

BEADS

SHAVING CREAM (MAKES "FLUFFY SLIME")

## MAIN INGREDIENT

WASHABLE SCHOOL GLUE (CLEAR)

WASHABLE SCHOOL GLUE (WHITE)

## SLIME ACTIVATORS

BAKING SODA

+

CONTACT LENS SOLUTION

LAUNDRY DETERGENT

OR

FABRIC SOFTENER

Chapter 7

# SLIME Management

**As of 2018, Garcia's videos had more than 1 billion views.** Because her videos remained popular, she continued to earn money from YouTube. In addition, Garcia has secured large **sponsorship** deals as well.

Sponsorship deals are often offered to YouTubers who have a lot of followers. Companies pay for their products to be shown or mentioned in a YouTuber's videos.

In this way, thousands of viewers will see or hear about the companies' products. Today, Garcia has sponsorship deals with Coca-Cola Company and Disney.

Many young slime makers use social media to help sell their creations. Some are so successful that they struggle to manage their time between the slime business and school!

Skyler Carmichael makes and sells slime in South Africa. But she has also sold and shipped more than 500 online slime orders to other countries!

Slime has brought a lot of value to Garcia's life. But she never sells the slime she makes. Once she finishes a batch, she puts the slime into food containers. Then she gives the slime to her younger **siblings**. They hand the slime out to friends. Or, they keep it for themselves!

Other slime makers do sell the slime they make, however. Many have created successful businesses doing so! Some of these **entrepreneurs** are very young and sell slime to their classmates at school. For example, Goldie Bronson is a fifth grader from Los Angeles, California. She sells small batches of slime for $5 each. One gallon costs $25.

Chapter 8

# SAFETY SCARE

**To make her recipes stand out, Garcia often adds fun ingredients like** glitter, beads, shaving cream, and paint. But slime recipes traditionally have three standard ingredients in common. Prior to 2017, those three ingredients were water, glue, and borax.

Borax is a household cleaning powder. It contains boric acid. This ingredient reacts with chemicals in glue to make slime stiffer and less sticky. Borax is called a "slime activator."

But borax also contains strong chemicals that can burn a person's skin. Because of this, slime recipes that call for borax also instruct users to **dilute** the powder in water. Diluting borax makes it less likely to cause burns.

Massachusetts slime maker Marli Perl uses liquid soap, lotion, and other ingredients in her slime.

In March 2017, an 11-year-old girl from Massachusetts was making slime with borax. She suffered serious burns. This caused concern in the slime-making community. For a time, many people worried that making slime at home was too **dangerous**. These concerns led to changes in the way slime is made.

Most slime recipes today no longer use borax. Instead, they call for safer ingredients. For example, contact lens solution can be used in place of borax. It contains boric acid but is not as toxic as borax. Today, Garcia uses contact lens solution instead of borax in all of her slime recipes.

Chapter 9

# WILD, WEIRD, and Wacky

As of 2018, Garcia's most viewed video is "100lbs of Slime!" This video currently has almost 25 million views! In the video, Garcia fills a giant, hollow ball called a Wubble Bubble Ball with huge quantities of slime. The ball becomes wobbly and difficult to control. Garcia tries to hold the ball in place. But the huge, soft, ball spills from her arms like a liquid!

Some experts say slime triggers a physical sensation called Autonomous Sensory Meridian Response (ASMR). ASMR is a person's positive reaction to certain sounds, sights, or touches.

Other popular videos of Garcia's include a recipe for an **edible** slime made with Starburst candy. Another shares a recipe for a fluffy slime made from

Slime makers have a lot of fun with color, texture, and ingredients in slime. They create slime that glitters, shines, wobbles, and more!

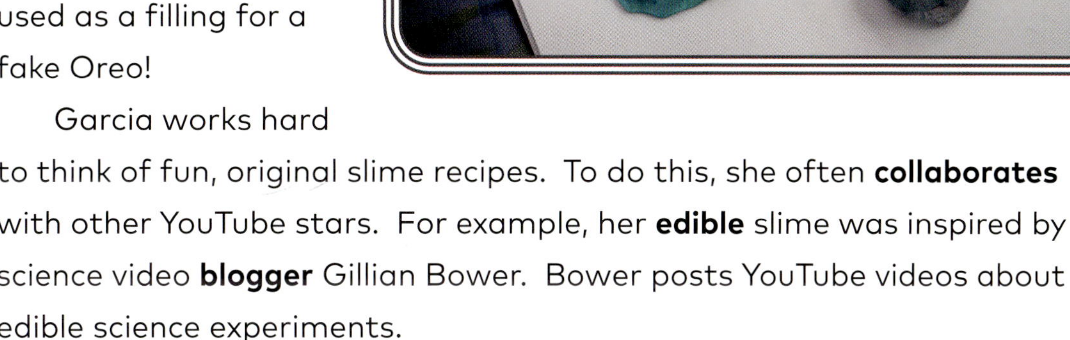

shaving cream. She even has a recipe for slime that can be used as a filling for a fake Oreo!

Garcia works hard to think of fun, original slime recipes. To do this, she often **collaborates** with other YouTube stars. For example, her **edible** slime was inspired by science video **blogger** Gillian Bower. Bower posts YouTube videos about edible science experiments.

Part of Garcia's success has to do with her creative recipes. But she is also known for posting videos showing wacky slime-making locations and activities. In one video, Garcia tries to make slime while **blindfolded**. In another, she makes slime while in a bouncy castle!

Chapter 10

# ON THE ROAD

**Garcia's passion for slime has contributed to her success. Fans can** see that she is enthusiastic about what she does! Garcia's lively personality shows through in every video she creates. It shows through in her live performances too.

In 2017, Garcia went on a tour around the United States. She visited 14 cities during August and September. The tour was organized by the **media** company Fullscreen Live. Fullscreen Live specializes in organizing events and tours for YouTubers and other **social media** artists.

While on tour, Garcia made a lot of slime on stage! She and other hosts also held fun challenges and competitions. Garcia spent a lot of time interacting with her fans while on tour too. She posed for pictures with attendees and took time to chat with them and sign their **merchandise**.

Near the end of her tour, in September of 2017, Garcia appeared on television. She was featured on *The Ellen DeGeneres Show*. She showed host Ellen DeGeneres and guest actress Reese Witherspoon how to make slime!

In addition to touring and appearing on television shows, Garcia has also been featured in many magazine articles about her slime success.

In October, Garcia appeared on the *TODAY* show. She shared recipes for making goopy green slime for Halloween. The same month, she **debuted** Craft City. It is a product line of craft materials. The brand has a website with tips and recipes, as well as information about Garcia.

Chapter 11

# LIFE BEYOND Slime

Garcia takes time to interact with her fans. She also takes time to give back to the people in her hometown. In December 2017, she visited her childhood neighborhood. While there, she gave food to others. She handed out burritos and a chocolate-based Mexican drink called *champurrado*.

Most of all, Garcia cares about her family. Growing up, she knew her father had always wanted a two-story house.

## FUN FACT

In December 2018, Garcia **donated** slime kits to a children's hospital. She said the experience was **humbling**. In the future, she wants to do more charitable work.

Raul Aguilar proposed to Garcia while standing in an arrangement of rose petals shaped like a heart.

Riverside, California, where Garcia and her family live

But the family could not afford one. In 2017, Garcia's slime success helped her make her father's dream come true.

Garcia bought a house worth $1.7 million in Riverside, California. The house has two stories and six bedrooms. Garcia lives there with four of her **siblings** and her parents.

In February 2018, Garcia's family grew. That Valentine's Day, Garcia's longtime partner, Raul Aguilar, proposed to her! Garcia posted a video of the proposal. And she has said she will video blog about her wedding planning on her personal YouTube channel.

Chapter 12

# MORE YET to Come

**Today, the slime trend shows few signs of slowing. Garcia posted a** new slime video on April 1, 2018. It was viewed more than 2 million times!

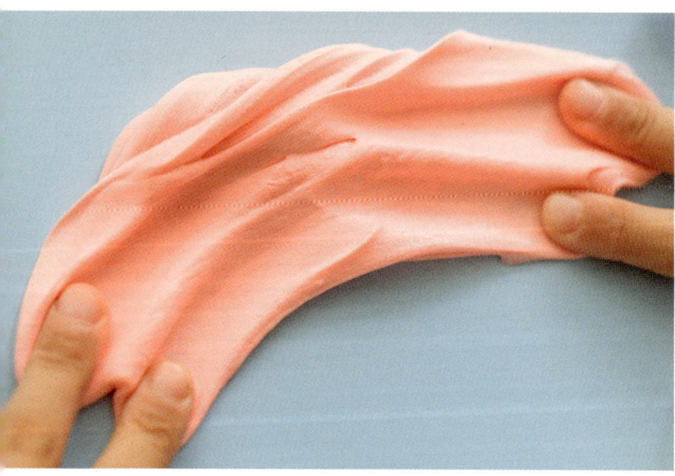

"Butter slime" is a recent slime trend. Air-dry clay gives this type of slime a creamy texture and allows it to be spread like butter!

Still, Garcia knows enthusiasm for slime may not last forever. She says she will be sad if the **craze** ends.

But Garcia is not worried about a future without slime. This may be because her work and influence now extend beyond slime.

Today, Garcia is an important figure in the Mexican-American community. *People en Español* magazine named Garcia one of 2018's most powerful **Latinas**.

Garcia spoke at the 2017 Foundation for Letters Gala in New York City. The event honors people who influence youth in a creative way.

Garcia's success would not have been possible if she had not followed her passion. Early in her career, people told Garcia that she was too old to be playing with slime. But Garcia continued doing what she loved.

Garcia's enthusiasm and persistence paid off! She is famous for her slime and craft expertise. Between 2017 and 2018, she even authored three books on these subjects!

Today, Garcia recommends that everyone start a YouTube channel. She insists that making videos can help people gain **confidence**. She also advises others to do what they love and follow their dreams.

# TIMELINE

### FEB. 1994

Karina Garcia is born in California.

### FEB. 2015

Garcia posts her first YouTube video, titled "Easy DIY Lipsticks!"

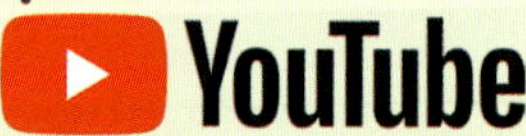


### AUG. 2015

Garcia posts her first slime video. In it, she makes a squishy slime that can be used as soap.

### SEPT. 2016

Garcia posts "100lbs of Slime!" It becomes her most-viewed video to date.

### 2017

Slime becomes a craze, and many people make their own at home using online recipes.

### MAR. 2017

An 11-year-old girl from Massachusetts suffers burns while making slime with borax.

## FUN FACT

Some slimes are thicker than others. But scientists consider all slime to be a liquid!

## AUG.–SEPT. 2017

Garcia goes on tour around the United States.

## SEPT. 2017

Garcia appears on *The Ellen DeGeneres Show*.

## OCT. 2017

Garcia launches a product line called Craft City.

## DEC. 2017

Sales of Elmer's glue, a popular ingredient in slime, doubles due to demand. Google announces "How to make slime" is the most searched how-to phrase.

## 2018

*People en Español* names Garcia one of the year's most powerful Latinas.

# Glossary

**available** – able to be had or used.

**balm** – an oily substance used for healing or protecting the skin.

**bankruptcy** – the state of having been legally declared unable to pay a debt.

**bath bomb** – dry ingredients hard-packed together and used to add essential oils, scent, bubbles, or color to bathwater.

**blindfolded** – wearing something, usually a strip of cloth, around the eyes to prevent or block sight.

**blogger** – a person who writes on a website that tells about their personal opinions, activities, and experiences.

**collaborate** – to work with another person or group in order to do something or reach a goal.

**confident** – having faith in oneself and one's powers. This faith is called confidence.

**craze** – an exaggerated enthusiasm that often only lasts for a short time.

**dangerous** – able or likely to cause harm or injury.

**debut** – to make a first appearance.

**dilute** – to make thinner by adding something else, often a liquid.

**donate** – to give.

**edible** – safe to eat.

**entrepreneur** – one who organizes, manages, and accepts the risks of a business or an enterprise.

**humbling** – causing a feeling of modesty.

**Latina** – a girl or woman born or living in Latin America, or a girl or woman of Latin-American origin living in the United States.

## ONLINE RESOURCES

To learn more about Karina Garcia and slime, visit **abdobooklinks.com.** These links are routinely monitored and updated to provide the most current information available.

**media** – a form or system of communication, information, or entertainment. It includes television, radio, and newspapers.

**merchandise** – goods that are bought and sold.

**sibling** – a brother or a sister.

**social media** – forms of electronic communication that allow people to create online communities to share information, ideas, messages. Facebook, Instagram, and Snapchat are examples of social media.

**sponsorship** – an arrangement where a person or organization pays the costs of a program or activity. In return, the person or organization receives promotion of a particular product or brand.

**subscribe** – to sign up to receive something on a regular basis. A person who does this is a subscriber.

**technology** (tehk-NAH-luh-jee) – machinery and equipment developed for practical purposes using scientific principles and engineering.

**texture** (TEHKS-chuhr) – the look and feel of the surface of something.

**tutorial** – instructional content that gives practical information about a subject.

**twin** – one of two children born at the same birth to the same mother.

# Index